CW01674219

young women

Julie Moser

EFFECTIVE
YOUTH MINISTRY
PRESS

Effective Youth Ministry Press
Visit us at: www.effectiveyouthministry.com

First published Australia 2008
First published North America 2010
Copyright © Julie Moser 2008

EFFECTIVE
YOUTH MINISTRY
PRESS

Scripture quotations taken from the HOLY BIBLE,
NEW INTERNATIONAL VERSION.
Copyright © 1973, 1978, 1984 by International Bible Society.

Apart from any fair dealing for the purposes of private study, research, criticism or review as permitted under the Copyright Act, no part of this book may be reproduced by any process without the written permission of the publisher.

Library and Archives Canada Cataloguing in Publication
Moser, Julie, 1965-
Studies for young women / Julie Moser.

Includes index.
ISBN 978-0-9811384-8-0

1. Christian women--Religious life. 2. Young women--Religious life. 3. Young women--Conduct of life. I. Title.

BV4551.3.M68 2009 248.8'43 C2009-903314-3

Graphic Design & Typesetting: Sarah van Delden
Edited: Belinda Hopper & Susie Ley

Printed in Canada

young women:

contents

leader's notes available through

www.effectiveyouthministry.com

Please don't photocopy these studies

all proceeds from the sale of this material goes straight back into youth ministry

young women:
introduction

Welcome to studies for Young Women!

It is great to be a young woman! However, there are so many struggles young women face that guys just don't understand. The world puts so much pressure on us to be attractive, sensitive, strong, gentle – there seems to be an endless list of expectations. However, the Christian young woman has a heavenly father who has spoken through His Word and provided guidance on how to live to please Him.

These studies single out just a few of the challenges that young women face and what the Bible has to say about each one. We will also read some Bible stories about some women who put their trust in God in our weekly personal Bible reading.

Enjoy being a young woman, but especially enjoy being a young woman who loves God and lives the way you were designed to. I hope these studies help you to understand how to do this.

Julie Moser

Young Women: Friendship

This is love: not that we loved God, but that he loved us and sent his Son as an atoning sacrifi
for our sins. 1 John 4:

let's get started

let's get started

1 What is something you enjoy about friendship with other girls?

2 What are some issues that can upset friendships between girls?
Look at the list below and rate in order of 1-6 what you believe to be the issues that cause tension in friendships between girls (1 is the biggest problem and 6 is the smallest problem).

- [ ] **Jealousy:** over a boy, clothes, possessions, talent, beauty etc.
- [x] **Fighting:** quarrelling and arguing about issues
- [x] **Betrayal:** friends not being able to keep a secret
- [ ] **Competition:** competing with one another unnecessarily
- [x] **Gossiping:** saying unkind or untrue things
- [x] **Stubbornness:** being unwilling to forgive and move on
- [ ] **Other?** ______________

Are any of these issues problems that you face with your friends?

Friendship is a great gift from God

Read Ecclesiastes 4:9-12.

How does this passage describe friendship?

What are the benefits of friendship listed in this passage?

- v. 9 ______________________________
- v. 10 ______________________________
- v. 11 ______________________________
- v. 12 ______________________________

Teaching on friendship

Write down what each of the following verses teaches us about friendship.

Proverbs 17:17

Proverbs 27:6

Proverbs 27:9

Would people who know you describe you as a good friend?

How are you a good friend? (For example, what do you do to show your friendship to others?)

Help, I need some advice!

What advice would you give to the Christian girls in the following situations? How can their Christian faith help them in each situation?

- Katrina's best friend is very possessive. She gets angry when Katrina spends time with other people.
- Olivia's group at school spends a lot of time gossiping about other people and sometimes she joins in.
- Jessica's feels really let down by a friend who failed to keep a secret.
- Natalie's friend is often moody with her and sometimes won't speak to her for several days without explaining why.

The Christian and friendship

The most important friendship we can have is friendship with God! **Read John 15:13** and **1 John 4:10**. How is friendship with God made possible?

____

____

How should being a friend of God (being a Christian) affect our friendships? (How can being a Christian make you a better friend?)

getting active

getting active

Helping each other

Go back to the list at the beginning of the study. Do you need to work on any of these issues in your friendships?

How can we help each other to be people who know how to be good friends?

let's pray

- Pray that we will be good friends to others.
- Pray that this group will show real friendship to each other.
- *Other things we can pray for*

____

____

stay tuned

Next week we will look at boyfriends and the kinds of relationships that honor God.

For your eyes only:
The week ahead

For your eyes only:

The Week Ahead

1. Personal Bible Reading

This week read the first five chapters from the book of Esther in the Old Testamer
This is the story of a young woman who God used to save her people.

My Weekly Bible reading Plan!

In Esther I read (place a ✔ when you have read it!)

Chapter 1 ☐ Chapter 2 ☐ Chapter 3 ☐ Chapter 4 ☐ Chapter 5 ☐

2. Memory Verse

Can you learn the memory verse at the top of the study (1 John 4:10)? Give it a t this week.

This is love: not that we loved God, but that he loved us and sent his son as an atoning sacrifice for our sins.

1 John 4:10

Pray for yourself that you will learn to be a better friend to others.

Think of the friendships you have and thank God for them.
Write down the names of three of your friends and pray for each one of them this week.

Friend 1. Ruth ______________________

Friend 2. Emily ______________________

Friend 3. ______________________

Living a life of love

Sometimes we don't know where to start when it comes to showing love to others. Romans 12:9-21 gives a practical list of ways we can show love. Read this passage and choose one action in the list that describes how to love each other, and try to work on it this week.

Young Women:
Boyfriends

Each of you should look not only to your own interests, but also to the interests of othe[rs]
Philippians 2

let's get started

let's get started

Complete the sentence:

I am old enough to have a boyfriend at the age of...

The age I think most girls start having sex is...

Most teenage guy/girl relationships end because...

The average length of time a girl/guy relationship lasts when you are a teenager is...

What are some positives about having a boyfriend?

What are some negatives about having a boyfriend?

going deeper

going deeper

Relationships that please God

Look at the following verses and describe the kind of relationships that God wants us to have:

1 Corinthians 6:18-20 ______________________________

1 Corinthians 13:4-7 ______________________________

Philippians 2:4 ______________________________

1 Thessalonians 4:3-7 ______________________________

How important is it to you to have a relationship that honors God?

How should a Christian couple behave differently from a non-Christian couple?

How important is it that your Christian faith influences this area of your life?

Read 1 Corinthians 7:39.
(A woman in Bible times had an arranged marriage, but if she was widowed she could choose anyone she wanted.) What instruction is given to someone who has the freedom to choose his/her own partner? What does this say to a Christian girl today?

Your value as a person comes from God

Your value must come from your relationship with God, not your relationships with the opposite sex. Have a look at the following verses:

God's loves you 1 John 4:10
When you believe in God you are his special child 1 John 3:1
God's plans for you are good Romans 8:28

When do girls feel the desire or pressure to have a boyfriend?

What can you and your Christian friends do to take away the pressure to have a boyfriend?

How do we pursue good friendships with the opposite sex, treating them in a way that honours Jesus and avoiding ways that dishonor Jesus?

Help, I need some advice!

What advice would you give to the Christian girls in the following situations? How can their Christian faith help them in each situation?

- Anne feels like there is something wrong with her because she doesn't have a boyfriend.
- Belinda has a new boyfriend and no longer spends time with her old friends.
- Catherine has broken up with her boyfriend. While she went out with him, she neglected all her old friends, so now they are angry with her and don't want to hang around with her anymore.
- Debbie is never single. As soon as she breaks up with her boyfriend, she finds another one.
- Evelyn has been going out with her boyfriend for a long time. They are finding it harder and harder to control the physical side of their relationship.
- Fran has sex with her boyfriend. She is worried that if she doesn't, he won't stay with her.
- Georgina is a Christian but dates non-Christian guys. She says, "It is not an important issue".

getting active

getting active

Helping each other

Is there anything that we must do differently in light of our study today?

How can we help each other to take the pressure off the need for a boyfriend?

let's pray

- Pray that our relationships with the opposite sex will be pure.
- Pray for contentment regarding having a boyfriend.
- Pray that we can help each other in our relationships with the opposite sex.
- *Other things we can pray for* ______________________________

stay tuned

Next week we will look at modesty and what God has to say about how we present ourselves.

For your eyes only:
The week ahead

For your eyes only:
The Week Ahead

1. Personal Bible Reading

This week keep reading the story of Esther

My weekly Bible reading plan!

In Esther I read (place a ✔ when you have read it!)

Chapter 6 ☐ Chapter 7 ☐ Chapter 8 ☐ Chapter 9 ☐ Chapter 10 ☐

2. Memory Verse

Can you learn the memory verse at the top of the study (Philippians 2:4)? Give it a try this week.

Each of you should look not only to your own interests, but also to the interests of others. Philippians 2:4

Pray that you will find your security in God and not in a boyfriend.
Pray that you may be pure in the way you relate to the opposite sex.
Pray for your friends who are in relationships right now.

Things that I can thank God for: ____________________

____

____

____

Things that I need to ask God to help me with: ____________________

____

____

____

Hot tips on relationships with the opposite sex

1. Go out in groups rather than just the two of you. Larger groups can be more fun than just two people together. This is also a wiser option and better for your other friendships.
2. Don't let your youth group become a place where everyone has gone out (romantically) with everyone else! Keep your relationships within your youth group at a friendship only level for as long as possible.
3. Try to avoid having a boyfriend through your earlier teenage years. Almost none of these last and break-ups can be painful and messy. The best thing for you and your guy friends is to wait!
4. If you do have a boyfriend, don't become so absorbed with each other that you neglect your friendships. Continue to go out in groups and invest in other friendships.
5. Don't be alone with your boyfriend to avoid being tempted to go too far physically.

Young Women: Modesty

Charm is deceptive, and beauty is fleeting; but a woman who fears the Lord is to be praised. Proverbs 31:3

let's get started

let's get started

1 Talk about what you are currently wearing and answer these questions:

- Why are you wearing what you are wearing? (i.e. comfort, to look good etc) looks good, comfy..
- Are you wearing any item you particularly like? jumper
- If you were dressing to go out with a guy, how would you dress differently? NO! wear the same things.

2 Circle "True" or "False" for the following statements, then discuss your answers:

Guys look at girls differently to how girls look at guys.	True False
Girls should dress modestly so that guys are not tempted to lust after what they see.	True False
If you wear revealing clothes you won't get a guy who is truly interested in who you are.	True False
God doesn't care if you wear revealing clothes.	True False

Beauty must come from within: **Read 1 Peter 3:1-6.**
What does this passage teach us about the way we are to dress?

Why is it so tempting to rely on our outward appearance?

Why is this wrong?

Have you ever met someone who appears attractive on the outside but was not attractive on the inside? How do you feel when you are around someone like that?

This passage does not mean that you should try to make yourself look physically unattractive. It does, however, teach that physical attractiveness is not what makes someone truly beautiful.

What are some occasions when you should try to dress nicely?

What are some times when you don't have to dress up?

Read Proverbs 31:30. What does this mean for a Christian girl today? (Can you give some practical examples?)

____

____

Dressing with modesty: **Read 1 Timothy 2:9-10.**
What does this passage teach us about how we are to present ourselves?

Write a list of what you consider to be acceptable as modest clothing. Share your list and discuss each item.

1. ______________________ 2. ______________________
3. ______________________ 4. ______________________
5. ______________________ 6. ______________________

Are there items of clothing you believe girls should not wear if they want to dress modestly?

What impression can a girl give to a guy when she wears revealing clothing?

What would you say to someone who wears revealing clothing to attract the attention of guys?

getting active

getting active

Helping each other

How can we help each other with the issue of dressing modestly?

Is there anything we need to change?

let's pray

- Pray that we can work on having a beauty that comes from the inside.
- Pray that we will honour Jesus in the way we dress.
- *Other things we can pray for* ____________________________________

____

stay tuned Next week we will look at honoring God in the way we speak about others and avoiding the problem of gossip.

For your eyes only:
The week ahead

For your eyes only:

The Week ahead

1. Personal Bible Reading

This week read the book of Ruth. Ruth was a young widow who left her home countr to care for her mother-in-law, Naomi. She trusted in God to provide for them an God didn't let her down. In fact, Ruth became an important part of God's plan o salvation and is counted among the ancestors of Jesus (Matthew 1:1-16).

My weekly Bible reading plan!

In Ruth I read (place a ✔ when you have read it!)

Chapter 1 ☐ Chapter 2 ☐ Chapter 3 ☐ Chapter 4 ☐

2. Memory Verse

Can you learn the memory verse at the top of the study (Proverbs 31:30)? Give it a try this week.

Charm is deceptive, and beauty is fleeting; but a woman who fears the Lord is to be praised. Proverbs 31:30

Pray that you can be a woman who relies on your inward beauty rather than your outward appearance.

Pray that you can be a woman like the one described in this week's memory verse (Proverbs 31:30).

Things that I can thank God for: ____________________

Things that I need to ask God to help me with: ____________________

Hot tips on how to dress modestly

1. Be careful with fashion, it comes and goes.
2. Try not to worry too much about what other people think; it is what God thinks that matters.
3. Help each other with the things you wear. Go through a list of fashion trends that may be immodest. These can include: pants that are so low they show the top of your backside, skirts that are so high they don't cover up enough when sitting down or bending over, tops that are so low-cut the focus is on your breasts, clothes that are too tight, clothes that have text on them that is suggestive or is inappropriate for a Christian.
4. Be prepared to be honest with one another about what each other wears. This means you also need to be prepared to listen to what is pointed out to you about what you wear.

Young Women:
Gossip

Do not let any unwholesome talk come out of your mouths, but only what is helpful for building others u according to their needs, that it may benefit those who listen. Ephesians 4:2

let's get started

let's get started

1 What is gossip? (Circle your answer)

...saying something about someone that is true	Yes	No	Unsure
...saying something about someone that is false	Yes	No	Unsure
...saying something about someone that is nasty	Yes	No	Unsure
...saying something about someone to make them look bad	Yes	No	Unsure
...sharing news that was meant to stay private	Yes	No	Unsure
...listening to someone say something bad about another person	Yes	No	Unsure

Discuss your answers.

2 When people around me gossip...

	Always	Often	Sometimes	Rarely	Never
I join in					
I tell them to stop					
I leave					
I listen but don't say anything					
I change the subject					

Which of the above do you wish you were able to answer differently?

Controlling the tongue. **Read James 1:26.**
What does this verse say about someone who gossips?

Read James 3:3-12.
Why is the tongue so powerful? (v. 5-6)

What is the trouble we have with our tongues? (v. 7-8)

Why must we control our tongues? (v. 9-12)

The problem with gossip
Look at the following verses and write next to each one why gossip is wrong:

Proverbs 11:13 ____

Proverbs 15:4 ____

Proverbs 16:28 ____

Are there times when it is OK to gossip? Why/Why not?

How can gossip hurt people? (Have you ever been hurt by others gossiping about you?)

Why is it hard not to gossip?

More teaching on gossip.

Write down the instructions each of the following verses gives about gossiping:

Psalm 34:12-14 ____

Proverbs 11:12 ____

Proverbs 20:19 ____

Proverbs 26:20 ____

getting active

getting active

Helping each other

What can you do the next time you are tempted to gossip?

What could you do when you hear others gossiping?

How can we help each other not to gossip?

let's pray

- Pray that we will be a group characterized by speech that honors God.
- Pray that we can keep a tight reign on our tongues.
- Pray that the way we speak about others will be a witness to those around us..
- *Other things we can pray for* ____________________________

stay tuned

Next week we will look at self-esteem and how we should view ourselves in light of our relationship with God.

For your eyes only: The week ahead

For your eyes only:

The Week ahead

1. Personal Bible Reading

This week try to read the book of Philippians, a letter written by the Apostle Pau whilst he was imprisoned. The theme of joy is very strong, which is quite extraordinar considering his circumstances.

My weekly Bible reading plan!

In Philippians I read (place a ✔ when you have read it!)

Chapter 1 ☐ Chapter 2 ☐ Chapter 3 ☐ Chapter 4 ☐

2. Memory Verse

Can you learn the memory verse at the top of the study (Ephesians 4:29)? Give it a try this week.

Do not let any unwholesome talk come out of your mouths, but only what is helpful for building others up according to their needs, that it may benefit those who listen. Ephesians 4:29

Pray for help in the way that you speak about others.

Pray that God will make you aware of the times you might gossip so that you can avoid it.

Pray that you will be someone who uses their words to encourage others.

Things that I can thank God for: ____________________

____

____

____

Things that I need to ask God to help me with: ____________________

____

____

____

Hot tips for controlling the tongue

1. Treat others how you would like them to treat you.
2. Learn to listen instead of speak – this is hard and takes practice.
3. Look for the positives in people.
4. Pray about controlling your tongue.
5. Ask a friend to help keep you accountable with what you say.
6. Make a commitment in this group to speak well of people and never to gossip. This includes prayer points – they cannot become a "godly" way to gossip.

Young Women:
Self Esteem

How great is the love the Father has lavished on us, that we should be called children of God! 1 John

let's get started

let's get started

What do you think?

Place a cross on the line below to indicate what you believe about the following statements:

	Disagree ------------------------ Agree
Most girls feel good about how they look	| -- |
Most girls are confident when talking with a guy	| -- |
Most girls are confident in a group	| -- |
Most girls are self-conscious about what they wear	| -- |
Having a healthy self esteem is important	| -- |
All Christian girls get their sense of value from God	| -- |

Place a cross on the line below to indicate how satisfied you feel about who you are. (If you feel comfortable, share your answers.)

Very unhappy with myself | -- | Happy with everything about myself

What are we worth? **Read Psalm 139.**

What does this Psalm tell us about how well God knows us? (vv. 1-4)

What do verses 7-12 tell us about God?

What do the following verses from this Psalm tell us about ourselves?

v.13 ______________________________

v.14 ______________________________

vv.15-16 ______________________________

Why do you think the person who wrote this Psalm is so angry with the people who hate God and misuse his name? (vv.17-24)

What does this Psalm teach us about our worth as human beings?

What do the following verses tell us about what we are worth?

Luke 12:22-24 and 31 ______________________________

2 Corinthians 5:16-18 ______________________________

Galatians 2:20 ______________________________

1 John 3:1 ______________________________

What makes us special?

What does the world teach us about what makes a person special?

Read John 3:16. What does the Bible say makes us special?

What can you do to trust what God says about your self-worth and avoid trusting what the world teaches?

The Story of Jane

Jane doesn't like herself very much. She is not able to acknowledge anything good about herself and doesn't believe she is attractive physically or personally. **How can you help her?**

NO!

getting active

getting active

Helping each other

How can we help each other have a Christian understanding of our self-worth?

How can we help each other when we struggle with our sense of self-worth?

let's pray

- Pray that we will be people who understand that our self-worth comes from God.
- Pray that we can help each other to remember who we are because of what Jesus has done for us.
- *Other things we can pray for*

stay tuned Next week we will have another great Bible study!

For your eyes only:
The week ahead

For your eyes only:
The Week ahead

1. Personal Bible Reading

This week try to read 1 John. This book has a strong theme of love, including God
love for us and our love for fellow Christians.

My weekly Bible reading plan!

In 1 John I read (place a ✔ when you have read it!)

Chapter 1 ☐ Chapter 2 ☐ Chapter 3 ☐ Chapter 4 ☐ Chapter 5 ☐

2. Memory Verse

Can you learn the memory verse at the top of the study (1 John 3:1)? Give it a tr
this week.

How great is the love the Father has lavished on us, that we should be called children of God! 1 John 3:1

Pray for help in the areas where you doubt your value in God's eyes.

Pray for a deeper understanding of God's love for you.

Things that I can thank God for: ______

______

______

______

Things that I need to ask God to help me with: ______

______

______

______

God loves you, He really does!

Read the following verses that speak of His love for you.

Romans 5:6-8

1 Peter 1:18-20

1 John 4:9-10

young women: driving!

and whatever you do, whether in word or deed, do it all in the name of the Lord Jesus, giving thanks to God the Father through him. Colossians 3:17

let's get started

Have you ever thought you were going to be in a car accident? What was the situation? How did you feel?

1 In most cities, car accidents are the most common way for young people to die. How do you feel when you hear this?

- ○ It won't happen to me!
- ○ I'll slow down for a while and then drive like a maniac again
- ○ I'm going to drive like a grandma after hearing this!
- ○ Something else? ________________

2 Why is it so tough to tell your friends not to drive too fast?

going deeper

going deeper

The Bible doesn't say a lot about automobiles (they usually walked back then!) However, there are some guidelines that we can follow.

Obey the law: Part 1! **Read Romans 13:1-5.**
What does this say about obeying the law?

____

____

Why is it so tough to obey the law in a car?

The speed meter is wrong.

How can we do a better job?

By not driving

Obey the law: Part 2! **Read Titus 3:1.**
How does this relate to being in a car?

____

____

How should we act when we drive together?

What happens if a passenger urges us to drive too fast or to drive recklessly?

Glorify God in everything you do! **Read Colossians 3:17.**
What does this verse tell us about how we should live?

____

____

How can we relate this to being in a car?

Helping each other

How can this group honor Jesus in the way we drive?

How can we help each other to drive safely?

think spot: 1

You're a passenger with a "crazed driver"! What should you do if you get into the car with a driver you are not sure of and they turn out to be a crazy driver?

- ◯ Grab the wheel and say, "I'm driving"
- ◯ Don't get in until you quiz them thoroughly
- ◯ Lie about your destination and get out early
- ◯ Talk to them about the way they are driving
- ◯ Close your eyes and think of a happy place
- ◯ Pray out loud
- ◯ Something else? ____________________

think spot: 2

What about aggressive driving? Why do some people seem to be so angry and aggressive when driving? How can we stay calm? Can you list 3 things that you can do to not get cranky behind the wheel? What should you do if you are confronted on the road by an aggressive driver?

let's pray

- Pray that we can drive in a way that honors Jesus.
- Pray that no one in this group will ever be harmed in an automobile accident.
- *Other things we can pray for*

____

____

____

For your eyes only:
The week ahead

For your eyes only:
The Week Ahead

1. Personal Bible Reading

This week choose a book from the Bible and try to read the whole thing.

2. Memory Verse

Can you learn the memory verse at the top of the study (Col. 3:17)? Give it a try th week.

And whatever you do, whether in word or deed, do it all in the name of the Lord Jesus, giving thanks to God the Father through him.
Colossians 3:17

3. Prayer

Pray that you will honor Jesus in all that you do.

Pray that this will happen in the lives of your Christian friends as well.

Things that I can thank God for: ______

______

______

______

Things that I need to ask God to help me with: ______

______

______

______

thank you

Thanks to Belinda Hopper and Susie Ley for their proofreading editing. Thanks also to Sarah van Delden for her work on the layout and graphics.

Other recommended resources for your youth ministry:

Small Group Bible Studies

Starting Out
By Ken Moser

Foundations For Christian Living
By Ken Moser

Young Men
By Ken Moser

Luke: Who is Jesus?
By Ken Moser

Luke: Jesus' Parables
By Ken Moser

Luke: Carry Your Cross
By Ken Moser

Death And Resurrection Of Jesus
By Julie Moser

Work Rest Play
By Ken Moser

Big Issues For Today's Youth
By Ken Moser

Studies 2 Go
By Julie Moser

More Studies 2 Go
By Julie Moser

Resources for Leaders

Programs 2 Go
By Ken Moser

Changing the World through Effective Youth Ministry
By Ken Moser

Creative Christian Ideas for Youth Groups
By Ken Moser

Youth Evangelism: Reaching Young People in a Way that Honours God
By Ken Moser

EFFECTIVE
YOUTH MINISTRY
PRESS

www.effectiveyouthministry.com